Enduring Hope

Finding Hope, Healing, & Freedom
On the Journey Home from War

Mark Buckman

Enduring Hope
Finding Hope, Healing, & Freedom On the Journey Home from War
Copyright by Get Free Stay Free, 2012
ISBN: 978-1475060201

Published by: **Get Free Stay Free**
                  2849 Laurel Park Highway
                  Hendersonville, NC 28739

Bible quotes found in this book are from the following versions:

The *King James Version* of the Bible.

The Holy Bible, New International Version. Copyright 1973,1978, 1984, by the International Bible Society. All Rights Reserved.

New American Standard Bible. Copyright THE LOCKMAN FOUNDATION, 1960, 1962, 1963, 1968, 1971, 1973, 1975,1977. A corporation not for profit. La Habra, California. All Rights Reserved

First Printing: 2012

Table of Contents

Introduction

My purpose in writing this book is multifaceted. First and foremost is to see our service men and women free from each and every effect of all Islamic curses prayed over them because of their faithful service to their country. Effects like depression, torment, PTSD, divorce, estrangement, and suicidal tendencies, just to name a few. As the son, grandson, great-grandson, nephew, brother and friend of soldiers, I have a deep and abiding respect for the dedication, service and sacrifice of our service men and women. While I have not always agreed with the choices that send them into harm's way, I will always unconditionally support these brave men and women who have sworn an oath to serve and protect my family, myself and my way of life.

Secondly, my desire is to equip fellow like-minded healing and deliverance ministries with the tools and insights needed to minister hope, healing, and freedom to emotionally and spiritually wounded veterans. I don't purport to be an expert in this arena, but simply offer our experience and the experience of fellow ministers to bring insight, understanding and focus to an area of great need.

In late September of 2009, my lovely wife Julie and I had the honor and privilege to work with a young Marine Reservist recently returned from a combat tour in Iraq. In preparing for his week of ministry, I began to research the issues facing veterans returning from OIF (Operation Iraqi Freedom) and OEF (Operation Enduring Freedom or the Afghanistan theater of war). What I discovered both broke my heart and focused my efforts.

According to V.A. (U.S. Veterans Administration) records, as of September 2009, 106,726 veterans of the wars in Iraq and Afghanistan have been diagnosed with mental health issues after leaving service. Of this number, 22% have been diagnosed with PTSD (Post-Traumatic Stress Disorder.) An article in *Air Force Print News Today* states,

"…the actual figure is probably higher. That number doesn't include troops still on active duty or veterans who have sought care outside VA channels. Many veterans don't come forward for fear that a mental-health diagnosis may harm their post-military careers; active duty members worry about being stigmatized or accused of malingering…" [1]

A quick word of warning and a disclaimer for the readers: Nothing I write in this book is meant to serve

---

[1] From the Web at: http://www.woundedwarrior.af.mil

as a medical or psychological diagnostic tool or treatment. I am not a doctor, psychologist, or licensed counselor. As a minister of the Gospel of Jesus Christ, led and directed by the Holy Spirit, I am presenting this material as a tool to deal with a **spiritual problem** affecting service men and women. If you are a Christian Healing and Deliverance Minister, then you are a safe alternative for veterans and active duty personnel who need freedom from the harmful spiritual effects of war.

Finally, it is my deepest hope and desire that the Church, the Bride of Christ, be better equipped to cover our service men and women in prayer. The Bible says, *"the effective prayer of a righteous man can accomplish much"*[2]. At the end of this book I have included a prayer focus for churches, small groups, youth groups, etc. to focus you and to help you be more effective in praying for our troops.

If you are reading this book and the concepts in it offend you, let me take a moment to say I'm sorry. Please put this book down and stop reading it. I didn't write it for you. I have no desire to dishonor or disrespect people of Muslim descent. The Bible tells us, *"we wrestle not against flesh and blood, but against principalities, against powers, against the rulers of the darkness of this world, against spiritual wickedness in high places."*[3]

---

[2] James 5:16, Holy Bible, New American Standard Bible
[3] Ephesians 6:12, Holy Bible, King James Version

It is my desire to expose the plans of our true enemy, satan, as he attempts to destroy the lives of young service men and women. Make no doubt about it, satan wants you to stay in darkness, and he wants his plans to go unnoticed. While my intent is not to delve into the beliefs and focus of Islam, we will be brushing over these topics from time to time.

"Finally, be strong in the Lord and in his mighty power. Put on the full armor of God so that you can take your stand against the devil's schemes."[4] Let's be strong for those who were strong for us. Let's step into our place of godly authority, equipping, and protection so we can stand in the gap for those who have stood so gallantly in the gap for us.

Mark D. Buckman

---

[4] Ephesians 6:10 & 11, Holy Bible, New International Version, Copyright © by Biblica

Assumptions

Ok so I'm gonna be brave and assume a few things about you the reader. Yes, before you ask, I'm fully aware of what 'they' say about assumptions and I'm not afraid to go there with you.

1. *I am going to assume that you are a Christian, that you at some point in your life have asked Jesus Christ to forgive you of your sins, and that you asked Him to be the Lord, the Boss, the Number One in your life. If this is not the case, I fear much of what you will read may sound like nonsense. My strong encouragement to you is to become a born again follower of Jesus Christ - part of God's family.*

2. *This leads to my next assumption, that you have at least a basic understanding of the concepts of spiritual warfare from a Christian world view. I also am going to assume that you recognize the existence of a literal devil and that his plan for you is to kill, steal, and destroy all that God wants to*

do in your life. I am assuming that you are open the possibility that things like curses and demonic torment aren't just the stuff of horror flicks, but are in fact tools used by the enemy against the followers of God. If not, I highly recommend two websites. The first is Restoring the Foundations ministry, www.restoringyourlife.org. The second is my website, www.getfreestayfree.com. Both will educate you and link you to resources to better equip yourself in fighting the good fight of faith.

3. *Finally I will assume you share the understanding that Islam as a religion is in no way compatible with Christianity. While I have always strived to show nothing but love, compassion and care for Muslims, I have no reason to apologize regarding my views and opinions of Islam. It is my sincere hope and prayer that the God of Abraham shine His light upon ALL the sons of Abraham so they can be made right with Him.*

These assumptions are meant to set the stage in your heart and mind for what you're going to read. They will also help keep me on track and away from rabbit trails of teaching things and exploring topics that other authors have covered so well.

Holy War, Batman!

"We're taking action against evil people ...our war is not against Islam.... Our war is a war against evil. This is clearly a case of good versus evil, and make no mistake about it -- good will prevail."
President George W. Bush, January 5th, 2002

"Why Iraq, Oh Muslims? Wake up. You're being attacked because of your religion. Iraq is being attacked for a number of reasons ... This is also a religious war"
Sheikh Ibrahim Mudeiris, March 21, 2003

There seems to be a great disconnect. On one hand we have world leaders declaring we don't have a problem with Islam or the Muslim faith and that we are NOT at war with Islam. On the other hand, Islamic religious leaders from all corners of the globe stand in their pulpits and cry out for jihad, for holy war.

So what's the big deal if on one side, the combatants view the struggle as a 'conventional war' and the other side views it as a 'holy war' or an attack on their way of life, their core belief, and values? Won't the outcome still the same? Won't the best funded, best backed group of armed forces still prevail? Won't the battles still be fought it the same way?

Well, yes and no. On one hand, the physical battle will be fought much like any other war. One army against the other army in battles with guns, bombs, planes, tanks, etc. So in that sense, these conflicts are like so many others in our long history. On the other hand, we can't ignore the religious and spiritual elements of this conflict.

The Bible is very clear regarding the nature of spiritual conflicts. In Ephesians chapter 6 we read, *"¹⁰Finally, be strong in the Lord and in his mighty power. ¹¹Put on the full armor of God so that you can take your stand against the devil's schemes. ¹²For our struggle is not against flesh and blood, but against the rulers, against the authorities, against the powers of this dark world and against the spiritual forces of evil in the heavenly realms."*⁵ If this war has a spiritual element, then what are these 'rulers' and 'authorities' saying? What is their battle plan for this war? What is their ultimate goal for our service men and women?

---

⁵ Ephesians 6:10-12, Holy Bible, New International Version

To better understand this issue, we need to take a look at what God's word, the Bible, says about the power of the spoken word.

*"¹ In the beginning God created the heavens and the earth. ² Now the earth was ⁽ᵃ⁾ formless and empty, darkness was over the surface of the deep, and the Spirit of God was hovering over the waters. ³ **And God said**, "Let there be light," and there was light."*⁶ Notice that the Bible doesn't tell us that God rolled up His sleeves, went to Creation Depot, filled up his cart, paid for it with His Master Card... Ok, I'll stop, but you get the point. It was with the spoken word that God brought everything into being: "And God said..."

We read in those first few chapters that we were created in God's image, and like God, we have been given the awesome power of speech. To quote Peter Parker's Uncle Ben in *Spiderman*, "with great power comes great responsibility." Personally I think the Spiderman folks were just ripping off Jesus when he said, *"From everyone who has been given much, much will be required."*⁷ In the Old Testament we read, *"Death and life are in the power of the tongue."*⁸ In the New Testament, James, while admonishing us to tame our tongues, says, *"With the tongue we praise our Lord and Father, and with it we curse men."*⁹

---

⁶ Genesis 1:1-3, Holy Bible, New International Version
⁷ Luke 12:48, Holy Bible, New American Standard Bible
⁸ Proverbs 18:21, Holy Bible, New American Standard Version
⁹ James 3:9, Holy Bible, New International Version

So let's consider this further; do unsaved people carry this same power of life and death in their tongues? Do they have the ability to speak "life" and "death" over people in the same way we as true believers do? Can the unrighteous "curse" the righteous? Does any of this even matter?

I want to take a minute to talk about curses. Derek Prince said this regarding curses: "Curses are words spoken, with some form of spiritual authority, that set in motion something that will go on generation after generation. Behind the words is a spiritual power: God or satan."[10]

In Genesis 4:7, God tells Cain something very interesting: *"sin is crouching at your door; it desires to have you, but you must master it."*[11] There is the idea of a 'door' that makes the concept of spiritual authority so interesting. On one hand God, is totally in charge of everything, and on the other hand, He allows us to make choices for ourselves.

God, the author and the finisher of life, gave us the right and the ability to open and shut the doors of our heart to the spiritual authorities of our choosing. It's especially interesting when you view 'authority' as the person, thing, or place you allow to have influence in and over your life.

[10] Derek Prince, *Curses: Cause and Cure,* Tape series no. 6011, Derek Prince Ministries
[11] Genesis 4:7, Holy Bible, New International Version

When we are born, we are under the authority of our parents. They have the responsibility to care for us physically and spiritually. It's our parents, or whoever. raises us, that determine whether or not we are going to church, praying at the dinner table, having home Bible studies, etc. They had the right, the responsibility, and the authority to make these choices for us when we were young, but then we grew up. Somewhere along the way we learn that even though we can venture further and further from under momma's apron, we still are under authority. Sunday school teachers, elders, youth pastors, and senior pastors all exercise a bit of spiritual authority in our lives, especially when we reach that point in our lives that we choose to listen to them and give them an open door into our lives.

You probably realize that other things can influence us spiritually as well. Things like music, games, sports, and even national pride often influence the choices, decisions, and attitudes that we have. How many of you, during lunch after a stressful morning at work meditate upon the chorus of that much revered Buffett/Jackson song, "It's Five O'clock Somewhere" and dream about kissing off the rest of the workday? How many of us widow and orphan our families during a sports season, or even just for that hour when 'my show' is on?

Places can also exert a certain amount of spiritual influence on a person who is open to it. Las Vegas knows this all too well and uses it in their very successful marketing campaign, "what happens in Vegas stays in Vegas." Tourism officials are capitalizing on the temptations of drunkenness, gambling and worse to attract people who will be "open" to what they have to offer. But sadly what happens in Vegas can, will, and does follow you home.

So what does war in Iraq & Afghanistan, curses, and spiritual authority have to do with each other? It all goes back to spiritual authority, the 'rulers' and 'authorities' that the Bible talks about, that are in force over the region. For starters, we know that both countries are predominately Islamic, so we know that the earthly 'spiritual authorities' don't have the same world view or even eternal view that Christians do. These authorities pray to a different god, practice a different religion, and strive for the world wide domination of Islam by any means necessary. These authorities, by their many words and deeds, have opened themselves and their regions up to being influenced by satan.

So does that mean God isn't in authority in these regions? Not at all, but the earthly authorities there have submitted themselves (and their people) to negative spiritual influences. They have given these influences place, purpose, and power in their region. The same way an individual can give satan an open door (authority) into his or her life, the earthly rulers of a place can open doors (give authority) to satan. Once satan has been given a place of authority over a region, then the stage is set for all hell to break loose.

So back to the reason we are here: our service men and women. The caliphs, mullahs, and sahibs from Gaza to Iraq to the corner mosque here in the U.S. are seeing these conflicts as an assault on Islam. "The aggression against Iraq is an assault on Islam, the Koran and the message of Muhammad"[12] was one of many such messages preached openly as far back as 2003. Sheikh Muhammad Abu Al-Hunud who gave this message on state owned television in Palestine finished up with this prayer: "Allah, purify the Islamic soil from the American and British treason and defilement...Allah, make their possessions a booty for the Muslims, Allah, annihilate them and their weapons, Allah, make their children orphans and their women widows."[13]

I could write a book full of Islamic sermon excerpts supporting this view of the conflict. They all use words like jihad (holy war or struggle), crusader invasion, and infidel when describing these conflicts and the non-Muslim people involved in them. So now that we know what these spiritual rulers and authorities are saying, what is their spiritual battle plan? In addition to encouraging Islamic men from all over the world to come to Iraq and Afghanistan to take up arms in this

---

[12] Preached by **Sheikh Muhammad Abu Al-Hunud** and broadcast on Palestinian Authority Television, March 28, 2003
[13] Preached by **Sheikh Muhammad Abu Al-Hunud** and broadcast on Palestinian Authority Television, March 28, 2003

struggle, Islamic religious leaders the world over are urging all devout Muslims to take up the call to pray.

These leaders urge, command, and cajole their flock into praying against our service men and women, their families, and their nations on a daily basis. This is not just an American problem. Britain as well as a few other countries are mentioned quite often by name in these prayers. This is a focused and sustained spiritual attack upon the non-Islamic service men and women faithfully serving their countries in these conflicts. The true enemy, satan, has blinded this people with a lie so effectively that they are focused, determined and steadfast.

What is satan's ultimate goal for our service men and women? It can be summed up in this quote, "we ask Allah to curse more American soldiers. In addition, we ask Allah to make the American soldiers realize that the only way out of the curse is to sincerely convert to Islam.... O Allah, curse them. Destroy the lives of each of these wicked soldiers. Make them taste humiliation in this life and the next."[14] Our armed forces have been deployed in conflicts the world over, but rarely have they faced such a direct spiritual assault with the stated goal of destruction in this life and in the life to come.

Don't be fooled by what the media, our leaders, or the Muslim shop owner down the street says. This IS a holy war and it is high time the people of God begin to

[14] On the web at: http://www.Islamonline.net

act like it. It is time for us to take up our spiritual arms. It is time for us to go on the offensive and take this fight to our REAL enemy – not Muslims, who we are commanded to love and pray for. To quote the Christian rock group Petra, "Get on your knees and fight like a man!"

Cause and Effect

"Do not be deceived, God is not mocked for whatever a man sows, this he will also reap"
The Apostle Paul, Book of Galatians 6:7

"Like a fluttering sparrow or a darting swallow, an undeserved curse does not come to rest."
King Solomon, Book of Proverbs 26:2

"I came that they may have life, and have it to the full."
Jesus Christ, Book of John 10:10

Now I'm not the kind of guy that goes around looking for the devil hiding behind every rock. Despite his claims to the contrary, the devil is just not that good. I don't like giving him credit where credit truly isn't due. But on the other hand, when the issue proves to be demonic in nature, I have no problem taking the battle back to his camp with a couple of holy hand grenades.

I also don't try to go all 'hyper-faith' when I open my mouth to talk. You know what I mean, don't you? Have you ever said something like, "dude I'm tired" after a 10 mile hike, and your hiking partner comes back with, "don't claim that over your life," and he proceeds to quote a scripture while splayed out on the ground next to you panting for breath?

Just to clarify, I truly believe in what Paul says in Philippians, *"I can do everything through Him (Christ) who gives me strength."*[15] I believe in speaking good things over myself, my family, the Church, etc., but I also believe in being real. King David was real with God and some of his worst days became the inspiration for the best selling blues songs (psalms) of all time.

So when I felt led to approach this whole subject of a curse on service men and women serving in Iraq and Afghanistan, I wanted to be balanced. I didn't want to slide off into fanaticism and fear, but I also wasn't willing to let the devil slip one past the Church.

If there is something valid to this idea of a curse, then let's expose it and deal with it in God's way. If not, let's move on and minister to the physical and emotional wounds caused by trauma of combat.

[15] Philippians 4:13, Holy Bible, New International Version

So What Are They Praying Anyway?

The following is an excerpt from a dua, or prayer, for the mujahedeen, or soldiers fighting in a holy war:

"O allaah, verily we ask you to disperse their (the enemy's) gunfire (upon our warriors) and to shake the ground from beneath their feet and strike terror into their hearts. O allaah, cripple their support and blind their vision and send upon them decay and disease. O allaah, divide them against one another and disperse their unity and strike heavy discord amongst their ranks, and make them flee to their destruction, and show us from amongst your wonders and strength that you mete out to them, and make an example of them for those who are heedless. O allaah, quicken their defeat and make their wealth war booty for the Muslims."[16]

Now this is just one example of many such prayers (curses) on the internet. (I encourage you to do your own search by typing in a complete sentence of this prayer into google.) They are often preceded with a line like:

"Brothers and Sisters: The greatest support you can give the Mujahedeen involves you raising your hands towards the heavens and making

---

[16] On the web at: http://www.anwar-alawlaki.com

rigorous supplication to Allah most high with the following dua"[17]

The faithful have even banded together and have produced handy little posters complete with all the words and a reminder to pray, pray, pray.

On www.islamonline.net, in an article entitled, "An Example of Allah's Curse upon a US Soldier," the author shares:

"This news item is an example of what happens when Allah's curse is upon the US Soldier... It can come in different ways; this just happens to be one of those ways which are the scariest. A huge percentage of US Soldiers are cursed with PTSD (post traumatic stress disorder)..."

He goes on to offer this supplication:

"...we ask Allah to curse more American soldiers. In addition, we ask Allah to make the American soldiers realize that the only way out of the curse is to sincerely convert to Islam."

Further down in this same article, the author continues his curses:

"O Allah, curse them. O Allah, curse them. O Allah, curse them.

---

[17] On the web at: http://www.militantIslammonitor.org

25 | P a g e

Destroy the lives of each of these wicked soldiers. Make them taste humiliation in this life and the next." [18]

Now to be balanced and fair, let me attempt to answer the critics who claim I am building a case against Islam based upon the ranting and ravings of a few isolated individuals. Let me share with you the historic source of these curses, the Koran.

On the next two pages, you will find seven categories of curses against non–Muslims that are found in the Koran. I have organized them and have compared them with the curses being prayed, preach and proclaimed over our military personnel and their families today.

---

[18] On the web at: http://www.Islamonline.net

Comparisons of Islamic Curses from the Koran and from Modern Prayers

Curses from the Koran	Modern Islamic Curses
Mental Torment Torment in this life Terror in the heart Tear out hair and go insane Misery	**Mental Torment** Strike terror/fear into their hearts. Shake the ground/earth from beneath their feet
Emotional Hardness Hard Heartedness Hatred Hostility Ill Will Animosity Antagonism Anger	**Emotional Hardness** Humiliation in this life and the next Make their plots turn against them Make their condition severe amongst themselves
Victimization & Abandonment Rejection Being Despised Disgrace Shame	**Victimization & Abandonment** Cripple their support Make their destruction a lesson for those who do not learn lessons
Attacks on Faith Rebellion Disbelief Bondage/slavery Torment till you turn to Islam	**Attacks on Faith** Blind their sight Blind their vision Make them flee to their destruction, Make the soldiers realize that the only way out of the curse is to convert to Islam

Curses from the Koran

Attacks on family & Unity
Division in the family
Children turning against parents
Your children become orphans
Your wives become widows
Loss of inheritance

Physical Attacks
Death
Crucifixion
Loosing hand or foot
Smite the neck, Fingers and toes
Boiling water poured over the head

Attacks on Provision, Possessions, and Abilities
Loss
Loss of inheritance

Modern Islamic Curses

Attacks on family & Unity
Disperse their unity
Divide them against one another
Strike heavy discord amongst their ranks
Disperse their gatherings and shatter their unity

Physical Attacks
Cripple their limbs
Blind their sight
Send upon them epidemics and calamities
Send upon them decay and disease.

Attacks on Provision, Possessions, and Abilities
Hasten their destruction
Make their wealth a bounty for the Muslims.
"We ask you to disperse their (the enemy's) gunfire (upon our warriors)
Scatter their aim

Digging in Deeper

So I want to go back to these 'prayers' that are floating around and dig in a little deeper. Let's look at two of the points from these prayers and compare them to news accounts of actual events from both the front lines and the home front. Together we will explore the negative effects that this one sided spiritual battle is having upon our service men and women.

Make Em' Miss

"Verily we ask you to disperse their (the enemy's) gunfire (upon our warriors)," Sounds harmless enough, come to think of it I would probably pray for bullets to miss me too, but another version of the same basic prayer points to the heart of the matter, *"Scatter their aim."* Instead of asking for the bullets not to hit them or for wisdom to know when to duck and cover, the supplicant is asking his or her deity to become involved in the fight, to intervene and interfere with the abilities of our service men to "service the target".

And their guns did fail:

> *"WASHINGTON – It was chaos during the early morning assault last year on a remote U.S. outpost in Afghanistan and Staff Sgt. Erich Phillips' M4 carbine had quit firing as militant forces surrounded the base. The machine gun he grabbed after tossing the rifle aside didn't work either.*

When the battle in the small village of Wanat ended, nine U.S. soldiers lay dead and 27 more were wounded. A detailed study of the attack by a military historian found that weapons failed repeatedly at a "critical moment" during the firefight on July 13, 2008, putting the outnumbered American troops at risk of being overrun by nearly 200 insurgents"[19]

The headline in the New York Times asked, "Are US Troop Weapons Duds?". Now I know that some of you out there are going to say, "Mark, guns jam, it's just a fact of life." No doubt, but this same report goes on to talk about another firefight, with eerily similar circumstances in which 8 servicemen lost their lives.

Make Em' Scared

"Shake the ground from beneath their feet and strike terror into their hearts." I don't know anyone, civilian or military, that can truthfully say that they have never been afraid in dangerous situations. We all were created with that God-given desire to NOT die. This specific curse speaks to a deeper level of fear and terror bent on shutting our service men and women down both emotionally and physically. As I mentioned earlier, Islamic prayer warriors see Post Traumatic Stress Disorder (PTSD) as a direct fulfillment of Allah's curses against our soldiers.

[19] Richard Lardner for the Associated Press, Published October 11th, 2009

And our soldiers are suffering:

"More than any previous war, the wars in Iraq and Afghanistan are likely to produce a high percentage of troops suffering from PTSD," due to the widespread use of improvised explosive devises, multiple rotations, the ambiguity of fighting combatants dressed as civilians, and the use of National Guard members and Reservists.

Dr Gerald Cross, who served as the undersecretary for health at the Veterans Health Administration during the Bush administration, testified in US District Court that of the 300,000 veterans of the Iraq and Afghanistan wars treated at VA hospitals, more than half were diagnosed with a serious mental condition, 68,000 of which were cases of PTSD.

Dr. Arthur Blank, a renowned expert on PTSD who has worked closely with the VA, testified that about 30 percent of Iraqi war veterans are likely suffering from PTSD[20]"

This article makes this dire prediction:

"Unless systemic and drastic measures are instituted immediately, the costs to these veterans, their families, and our nation will be

---

[20] Excerpts from: "60,000+ Iraq, Afghanistan Vets Diagnosed With PTSD" by Jason Leopold. Found on the Web at: http://www.scoop.co.nz/stories/HL0803/S00119.htm

incalculable, including broken families, a new generation of unemployed and homeless veterans, increases in drug abuse and alcoholism, and crushing burdens on the health care delivery system and other social services in our communities. "[21]

Where Do We Go From Here?

While I could spend several more pages sharing heart breaking story after story, I want to us to shift into action. While it may be a fact that the true enemy of our souls, satan, can and often does attempt to curse us and afflict us with misery, sadness and sorrow, I want us to focus on the Truth. I am talking about the timeless Truth that we were created for a life of freedom and abundance. Jesus sums it up by saying, *"The thief (*that would be satan*) comes only to steal and kill and destroy; I have come that they (*that would be YOU*) may have life, and have it to the full."* [22]

---

[21] ibid
[22] John 10:10, Holy Bible, New International Version

Foiling the Curse

"Curses are words spoken, with some form of spiritual authority, that set in motion something that will go on generation after generation. Behind the words is a spiritual power: God or satan."
Derek Prince.

"With the tongue we praise our Lord and Father, and with it we curse men...My brothers this should not be"
The Apostle Jame, James 3:9 & 10

"The tongue has the power of life and death..."
King Solomon, Proverbs 18:21

Growing up, we were all told that thing about the sticks and stones and how they could wound us much worse than words ever could. Well, someone lied. Thankfully Jesus came to heal us of both external and internal hurts and wounds.

In His first official sermon, Jesus opened up the scroll to what we call Isaiah 61 and he shared, *"The Spirit of the Sovereign Lord is on me, because the Lord has anointed me to preach good news to the poor. He has sent me to bind up the brokenhearted, to proclaim freedom for the captives and release for the prisoners".* [23]

One of the more interesting things about being a follower of Jesus Christ is this concept of both spiritual and emotional freedom. Don't get me wrong, I love physical healing and freedom from ailments and diseases. But to be honest with you, I get just plain excited over this idea that Jesus came to fix our internal brokenness and set us free from our spiritual bondages. While I see the challenges facing our armed forces because of their faithful service in the Middle East, I am convinced that God has already paved the way for these men and women to walk in total and complete wholeness.

In 2009, the Lord began to put these service men and women on our hearts. As we began to seek the Lord's wisdom on what to do, we knew that a prayer had to be crafted to assist ministers, counselors, soldiers, and family members in breaking these war curses. The resulting prayer is offered here as one of the steps in a larger journey towards complete healing and restoration.

---

[23] Isaiah 61:1, Holy Bible, New International Version.

I want to encourage you to read over, understand and agree with this prayer before you decide that this step is right for you. Take the time to ask God for His wisdom. When it's time to break these curses, get yourself in the right frame of mind AND spirit. Take this to heart: You're not merely reading rote words on a page; you are going to battle. Pray this prayer with the same focus, determination and drive you had while deployed.

Make sure to pray out loud. Our true enemy, satan, is using the power of spoken words to proclaim and call down curses openly and boldly on a daily basis. Walk in the authority God has given you as His son or daughter and claim your freedom as you proclaim this prayer out loud.

Prayer for Breaking Islamic War Curses from Service Men & Women

Heavenly Father, I acknowledge that during my time of military service to my country, I was deployed to and involved in Operation Iraqi Freedom and/or Operation Enduring Freedom (OIF/OEF).

Lord, I choose to forgive every officer and leader in authority who gave me orders to commit any sin during my military duty. (Be Specific)

Lord I choose to forgive everyone else who encouraged me to enter into any sinful activity or behavior that was supposed to help me deal with the stressful effects that combat had on me. (Be Specific)

Lord, I choose to confess all my sinful behavior associated with OIF/OEF. (Be Specific).

Heavenly Father, I ask You to forgive me for everything sinful I did and to cleanse me from every unrighteous act I committed as a result of my military duty in OIF/OEF.

Lord, I receive Your forgiveness and I thank You for cleansing me of any and all unrighteousness.

Father, in the basis of Your forgiveness, I choose to forgive myself for any sinful behavior I engaged in during my time serving in OIF/OEF and since I have returned home. I will no longer hold myself guilty because I know that You have forgiven me.

Father, in the Name and on the Authority of Jesus Christ, I stand in faith and renounce and break the power of every evil word that was knowingly or unknowingly spoken against me by any other person, cult, group or religious leader.

I renounce, break and cancel the power of each and every curse assigned to me, in the Name and on the Authority of Jesus Christ.

I renounce and break all curses of mental torment, including all terror, fear, insanity, misery, self-inflected injuries, torment, depression, and any and all effects of post traumatic stress disorder. I rebuke every demon sent to torment me by masquerading as a human spirit ('haunting') and I command them to go and leave me now, based upon the finished work of Christ on the Cross and my authority as a believer.

I renounce and break all curses of emotional hardness, including all hard heartedness, stuffed emotions, hostility, ill will, animosity, antagonism, anger, rage and hatred, including all hatred and rage against Muslim people.

I renounce and break all curses of victimization and abandonment, including all rejection, disgrace, humiliation, shame, discord, and disunity. I declare that

I will not be used as an example and that I will not be abandoned by my support.

I renounce and break all curses placed upon my faith, including all rebellion, disbelief, religious bondage, slavery, loss of vision, loss of purpose, and all torment that would cause me to turn to Islam. I break agreement and renounce the lie that the only way I will be free from this curse is to turn to Islam. I declare that I will not abandon my faith and flee towards my own destruction.

I renounce and break all curses placed upon my family, including division in the family, the rebellion of children against parents, heavy discord, disunity, and loss of inheritance. I declare that my children will not become orphans and my spouse will not be widowed by my physical death, emotional hardness or by blocked emotions.

I renounce and break all curses placed upon my provision, my possessions and my abilities, including all loss, loss of inheritance, destruction, looting, and all attacks upon my giftings, talents, and abilities.

I declare that the power of these and all other curses spoken over me because of my service in Operation Iraqi Freedom and/or Operation Enduring Freedom are broken. I speak death to the seeds of destruction that were sown into my life.

Father I ask You to heal my mind, my emotions, my physical body and my family. Father, I ask You to strengthen my faith and to surround me with the knowledge and understanding that as your son, I have never been and never will be abandoned, forsaken or alone. Father I ask you to restore every possession, form of provision, and ability that was damaged or stolen from me or my family.

Father I thank you from freeing me from these curses and for restoring and healing all satan has tried to steal from me and my family. All this I pray in the precious name of and on the unquestionable authority of Jesus Christ. Amen.

Please Note: This Prayer Can Be Downloaded in Printable Form from: www.getfreestayfree.com/enduringhope

Raising the Shield

During times of armed conflict, opportunities seem to arise almost daily for us to show admiration and support for our troops. It is vital to the moral of our brave service men and women and their families to know that we are standing behind them.

As we continue to take every opportunity to bless our troops by meeting physical needs and wants, I urge you to do your part in meeting their spiritual needs as well. The following Prayer Focus has a two-fold purpose:

1. To provide a spiritual shield or covering for our troops and their families from the emotional, spiritual, and physical effects of these wars.

2. To open the door for these men and women to find safe places of hope, healing, and restoration once they do return home.

Bless you and thank you for doing your part to cover and support these brave men and women.

Prayer Focus for Service Men and Women Serving in Islamic Regions

Note: The following prayer points are meant to serve as suggestions and reminders of what to pray while praying for our troops. As always, when you are praying, allow the Holy Spirit the permission and the right to lead, guide, and direct what you pray.

Prayer Points for Physical Protection

Pray for protection and freedom from as well as for all spiritual doors being closed to:

Physical injury and trauma including:
Death, epidemics, calamities, decay and disease
Loss of or crippling injuries to the limbs, hands, feet, fingers or toes
Injuries to or attacks upon the head, neck, or eyes

Loss of personal property, income, savings, or wealth through destruction, looting, divorce, theft, trickery, deceit, or any loss of inheritance.

All attacks against a soldier's gifts, abilities, talents and skills.

Pray for our soldiers to be blessed with divine health, physical protection, and complete protection for their gifts, abilities, talents and skills.

Prayer Points for Emotional Protection

Pray for protection and freedom from:

Mental torment including:
Terror, fear, insanity, misery, self-inflicted injuries, depression, and all effects of post traumatic stress disorder.

Emotional hardness including:
Hard heartedness, stuffed emotions, blocked emotions, hostility, ill will, animosity, antagonism, anger, rage, and hatred, including all hatred and rage against Muslim people.

Pray for our soldiers to be blessed with wisdom, emotional stability and strength, spiritual peace, spiritual rest. Pray protection over their mind, will, and emotions.

Prayer Points for Spiritual Protection

Pray for protection and freedom from:

Attacks upon faith including:
Rebellion, disbelief, spiritual bondage, spiritual slavery, doubt, double-mindedness, loss of vision, hopelessness, helplessness, spiritual blindness, or abandonment of faith.

Demonic and occult influences including:
Demonic torment, harassment, and curses.

Pray for our soldiers to be strengthened in their faith, for them to connect with God in a real and personal way. Pray for them to receive and walk in a spirit of sonship, and for them to grow in the wisdom, knowledge and understanding of the Lord. Pray for revival to break out amongst our military personnel. Pray for spiritual protection from every fiery dart launched at then and from every evil scheme planned against them.

Prayer Points for Military Families

Pray for protection and freedom from:

Attacks upon family life including: Rebellion of children against parents, heavy discord, disunity, divorce, separation, loss of inheritance, orphanhood, widowhood.

Pray for marriages and families to be strengthened through better unity, communication, understanding and emotional intimacy.

Please Note: This Prayer Focus Can Be Downloaded in Printable Form from: www.getfreestayfree.com/enduringhope

Enduring Hope

Life is a journey full of twists and turns, highs and lows, good days and bad. Your unique story reveals the people, beliefs and events that have mapped out your life's course. It's the good days and beautiful things that remind us of God's plans and His great love for us. But it's often the wrong turns, misguided wanderings and the ten car pile ups that determines life's course.

If your life is stuck, broke down, or just off track and you're ready to experience real hope, healing and freedom, we're here to help.

Get Free Stay Free Ministries
www.getfreestayfree.com

We pray and hope for God's richest blessings on you and your family as you journey towards the abundant life He created you to live.